That's Life...

41 Life Challenges and How to Handle Them

Tim Connor, CSP

**Executive
Books**

That's Life

ISBN: 0-937539-57-0

LCCN: 2001090907

Published by **Executive Books**
206 West Allen Street, Mechanicsburg, PA 17055
www.ExecutiveBooks.com

Cover Design: Melissa Lingle

Editor: Kristen Boykin

First Printing: June 2001

To reach Tim Connor, CSP:
Voice: 704-895-1230   Fax: 704-895-1231
E-mail: Speaker@bellsouth.net
Website: www.timconnor.com
Mail: Box 397, Davidson, NC 28036

Manufactured in The United States of America

*"If you are strong enough,
there are no precedents."*

F. Scott Fitzgerald

"May the roads rise to meet you,
May the winds be always at your back,
May the sun shine warm upon your face,
The rains fall soft upon your fields,
And until we meet again,
May God hold you safely
in the hollow of his hand."

Irish Blessing

Books by Tim Connor, CSP:

- Soft Sell
- Win-Win Selling
- The Voyage
- Sales Mastery
- The Trade-Off
- The Ancient Scrolls
- Crossroads—A Love Story
- How to Sell More in Less Time
- Daily Success Journal
- 52 Tips for Success, Wealth, and Happiness
- Walk Easy with Me through Life
- Your First Year in Sales
- That's Life
- Lead, Manage, or Get Out of the Way
- The Road to Happiness is Full of Potholes
- The Road to Happiness is Full of Potholes Fun-Book
- Assignment Workbooks:
    Sales
    Relationships
    Success
    Customer Service
    Management
- Let's Get Back to Basics:
    Success
    Life
    Happiness
    Sales
    Relationships
    Management

Contents:

"The greatest mistake you can make in life is to be continually fearing you will make one."

Elbert Hubbard

Introduction:

The only thing in life that is certain is its uncertainty. You can either learn to embrace the unexpected and release the expected, or live with a great deal of frustration, anxiety and stress.

Life for everyone can be either a joyous adventure, or filled with struggle, pain and adversity. Life is a neutral process that does not select some people for success and others for failure, some for happiness and others for loneliness, or some for wealth and others for poverty. Life comes to each of us one day at a time, and we make choices and decisions that create our outcomes and consequences.

Some of these outcomes may at first appear positive, but over time we learn that they had negative lessons. Others at first may seem to be negative, but with the passage of time bring positives that we never could have anticipated.

Many would argue that bad things happen to good people and good things happen to bad people. I would argue first that all of this depends on your definition of bad and good. What can seem to be bad for us (loneliness, for example) can bring us growth, peace and surrender in the end if we can learn to see the good in solitude. What can seem to be good for us (wealth for example) can bring us fear, arrogance and isolation.

The premise of this book is that every life has its share of opportunities, struggles, successes and failures, and that, regardless of what you may be experiencing at any given moment in your life, it can be either positive or negative depending on:

1- How you feel about it.
2- How it makes you feel about yourself.
3- What you do with it or about it.

It is not the premise of this book that everyone can—or should—experience the same type or degree of anything in life—i.e. happiness, success, fear or ignorance. That is not for me, or any other person, to wish for you or to expect life to take from you. We are each here to learn, grow and experience life – whatever form it takes for each of us—as we move through the days and years of our lives.

This book is not about answers to your needs, questions, struggles or dreams. It is about asking you to think differently or uniquely about whatever life has put in your lap at any given moment (either suddenly or over time)—whether it is perceived as good or bad, and whether it lasts for a fleeting moment or for many years.

In the end, each of us has the power to choose. Even a prisoner or servant can choose what fills his mind and spirit. Being free is not just a physical idea, but also a mental one. There are many people who have the ability to get in their car and drive across the country, but are afraid to leave the safety of their own living room.

This book is about freedom. The freedom to:

- believe
- change
- understand
- let go
- begin again
- enjoy
- accept
- feel

Each of the forty-one concepts was selected from my thirty-plus years of experience working with groups and individuals worldwide as a speaker, trainer and consultant. I am sure others could have been included, and you may wonder why some are included. I have found these to be the major reasons why some people struggle with life and others seem to enjoy every passing day regardless of what it brings.

The concepts are in no particular order of importance. I urge you not to just read them, but to read them *carefully* and to think about how they relate to your life and to your future.

Do you want anything in your life to be different or better than last year or yesterday in any way? Do you want greater success, more peace, less stress, more friends, more financial freedom, more fun, or _____ (add your own)?

What are you going to do different this year than last? Today versus yesterday?

Are you going to work harder or smarter?
Are you going to learn more?
Are you going to communicate more honestly?
Are you going to _____ (whatever)?

There is one sure way to guarantee that your dreams will be realized. There is one thing you can do, starting now, to ensure that the mistakes and lessons of last year are used as stepping stones to a better future. There is one action you can take now that will create a year in your life that is filled with happiness, achievement, success and prosperity.

Learn to control your thoughts!

The highest reward for a person's toil is not what they get for it, but what they become by it."

John Ruskin

Limitations:

It has been said by many people smarter than myself that "the only limitations we encounter in life are those self-limiting ones we place on ourselves." If this is true, then why do so few people reach their full potential? Why do so many people feel stuck, out of control and without hope in their lives? Why do so many people give up, quit, settle, resign themselves or operate out of blame, anger, guilt, resentment and self-pity in regards to the quality of their life?

If this question were answered in a book by the same title, it would never sell. Why? Because the very people we are talking about here do not want to take the responsibility for their lives. They insist on pointing a finger toward something or someone else for the cause of their station or circumstances in life.

I have been at the bottom of the barrel a few times in my life. I have also reached the mountaintop. I have met thousands of people who believe they do not have any choices. They are stuck in a job, business, relationship, way of life, neighborhood, climate or career. You and I are not trees. We can change what we do not like. Then why don't we?

The truth is—and I didn't just invent it or discover it—each of us came into this world headed for greatness in some way. We were engineered for success at birth and conditioned for failure along the way. We have forgotten our heritage. We have the most magnificent organ ever created in our skull— a mind that can create whatever it chooses. There is nothing we cannot do. The skeptics out there are thinking, "Sure, Tim. I can fly."

I do not have the time or the interest to deal with skeptics or critics. If that is their attitude, I will bet they take it into other areas of their life as well. This is not about you or me flying, but realizing we can do whatever we put our minds to, as long as we put action into our dreams. Certainly there are physical limitations in many areas or with some people. My only point here is that we could do more if we would only learn that our ceilings are self-imposed.

What mental images are you holding in your consciousness that may be holding you back? Is it the fear of failure or success? Is it the fear of rejection or public scorn? Is it an inner feeling of unworthiness? Or is it some other emotional issue or scar that you have failed to recognize or deal with?

*"Make the most of yourself,
for that is all there is for you"*

Emerson

Unhappiness:

Happiness! Everyone wants it, searches for it, dreams of it and longs for it. Unhappiness—no one wants to be unhappy. Are you happy? Really happy? If so, why? If not, what will it take for you to find and keep this elusive, yet seemingly attainable, state?

I have been miserable. I have been happy. And I have spent time in that limbo state of wanting to be but not knowing how to be.

Happiness is not a thing, address, possession, bank balance, or life position (retirement, marriage, being single, parenthood, etc.). It is not something you can grasp, earn, keep, buy, learn, give away or know. Happiness is not anything that you go after. It will come after you relentlessly if you have that inner state or consciousness that says, "I am happy no matter what is in my life."

This does not mean to imply that you will be happy 24 hours a day, 365 days a year. That would not be life as it was designed to be. It would also be exhausting! However, we were meant to be happy as a life destiny. Pain, grief, sadness, solitude, and, yes, even loneliness are all valuable contributors to a humble, joyous, compassionate, loving, balanced and productive life.

You cannot totally experience the thrill of victory without ever tasting defeat. You cannot completely bask in the sunshine of success if you have never been brought to your knees. And you cannot know fully the joy of a happy disposition, spirit and demeanor without ever knowing unhappiness.

Life is a wonderful adventure—filled with every imaginable

emotion, experience, test, adversity, achievement, mistake, and success. Life is not, nor will it ever be, perfect. Life is not a dress rehearsal for some later event. Life is now; what is happening now, what you are experiencing now, what you are learning now, what you are doing now, what you are dreaming now, and what you are afraid of now.

"*Happiness is neither within us only, or without us; it is the union of ourselves with God.*"

Pascal

Loneliness:

There is a significant difference between being lonely and being alone. Loneliness is caused by a deficiency of the spirit—a spirit that needs people or activity with regularity in order to feel a sense of worthiness, belonging or acceptance. Being alone can be seen as a positive opportunity to get to know yourself better while growing in wisdom, understanding and maturity.

The highest form of being alone is solitude. This is the time in life when you search out and choose to be alone.

Many people are alone out of choice, while others face this challenge due to a loss of a loved one or other circumstances. I have felt the sting of loneliness, and I have known the joy of solitude. The key is to understand the difference and realize its impact on your life and outcomes. I have known the heartache of loss and the peace of aloneness. There are four things you can do if you find yourself alone:

1. Use the time to get in touch with who you are, what you want, and what you believe.
2. Accept this time as an opportunity for creative growth.
3. Know that all things pass—even the pain you are feeling.
4. Do something new. Try a new activity, reach out to others, learn a new skill or spend time with others who face the same circumstances. Take a course or class in some thing.

Feeling sorry for yourself during this time will only make the time pass more slowly and with a greater degree of pain. Get busy, get started, and you will be amazed at how you can use this time for good—for yourself or for others.

There is a reason why you are alone—nothing in this life is

an accident. I know this may be difficult for you to accept if you have lost the love of your life—but believe me, suffering in silence will not help.

"God is ready the moment you are."

E. Fox

Disappointment:

Disappointment in life is directly related to your expectations. When you want something and expect to have it, achieve it or experience it, and it doesn't become a reality, then you feel let down, upset or disappointed. Why do people set themselves up for disappointment by creating mental expectations for some result that may be in the control of others: parents, a spouse, a company, a boss or a friend?

It is natural and normal to want something you don't have. To desire to achieve something you have yet to accomplish. To accomplish some task or enjoy some special status, recognition or power. It is not natural, however, to get everything you want in life. You can have almost *anything* you want—if you are willing to pay the necessary price (both short and long term) for it. But you can't have *everything* you want! It's just not that kind of world.

Disappointment is a part of life.

When you were young, if you were not permitted by your parents or caregivers to be disappointed, I guarantee that sooner or later you will experience a truth life wants you to learn—everyone experiences disappointment at some point (and some people more often than others). No one is immune. You cannot escape it, you can only learn to manage it.

Since disappointment is directly related to your expectations, what can you do to ensure that you are disappointed less in your life? You can:

1. Balance you optimism with your pessimism as you look at your expectations.
2. Accept the simple fact that you won't get every thing you want.
3. Learn to enjoy what you have and feel gratitude for having it.

"There is in the worst of fortune the best of chances for a happy change."

Euripides

Discouragement:

Have you ever wanted to quit? Anything? What is the cause of discouragement? Is it a sense of loss? Of feeling out of control? Loss of faith in yourself or the future? Is it feeling that your present circumstances will never end? I can only tell you that this emotion—more than most other emotions—will drain your creativity, purpose and resolve.

I have known discouragement more often than I like to admit. I can also tell you that something within me pushed to try again, try harder or take just one more step into the future—knowing that, if I gave in to this debilitating feeling, I would lose control of my life. Discouragement is a signal that something is wrong, something in your life needs to change. You can pay attention to its warning signs and find another way to approach whatever is causing your pain, or you can choose to whine.

The one thing which has helped me more than any other is my faith in God and the knowledge of his continuous love and acceptance. I have known deep in my soul and heart that what was happening was necessary for me in order to make a change in my life. It was His way of guiding me to a better tomorrow. It was not meant to break me, but to show me a better path. For many years, I ignored this guidance—feeling that I could do anything on my own with no help. As I matured and grew, however, I came to learn and accept that we all need help from somewhere sooner or later.

People will often let you down in your time of need. There is one guiding truth we all must learn if we are to overcome the feelings of loss of control—we are all on God's path to perfection, and we will all make mistakes traveling that path. Sometimes we need a gentle urging, and often we need a 2 x 4 across our foreheads.

If you are discouraged today about anything, know that this discouragement is in your life for your higher good. I know while you are in the depths of despair that this is a difficult request, but it is one you must accept.

"Pure motives do not ensure perfect results."

Bovee

Loss of Purpose:

Loss of purpose is akin to a loss of faith or patience as it is unfolding. It is a feeling that no matter what you do —it will not be good enough or soon enough. There are nagging questions, which keep popping into your consciousness. They scream:

What are you going to do with the rest of your life?
What are you doing with your life now?
Why aren't you further ahead in some area of your life?
Why haven't you accomplished more?

Purpose is the single most important motivator in a person's life. It keeps you keeping on when all around is caving in before your eyes—when nothing seems to work—when people have abandoned you and life seems to have forgotten your existence.

There is no easy way to regain your purpose. It is a function of many elements: will, desire, resolve, faith and trust. The way to discovering or re-discovering your purpose takes time, effort, passion, patience, contemplation, self-evaluation and commitment. These traits are not inborn or easily acquired, but, in the end once you own them, there is nothing that can stand in your way as you move into the rest of your life.

The first step in discovering (or re-discovering) your purpose is to find what you love. Find what you are passionate about, what you would spend your life doing regardless of payment. Most people live their lives hoping for something better, but refusing (or not knowing how) to do the necessary work on themselves in order to discover their purpose. I didn't discover mine until my late 30s—after reading dozens of books and asking myself numerous questions. Finally, after hundreds of hours of honest self-appraisal, it came to me—I wanted to help people with what I had learned in my life journey. This led to my speaking and training, and eventually my writing.

It won't be easy, but it will be worth the effort, believe me.

"I find the great thing in this world is not so much where we stand, as to what direction we are moving."

O.W. Holmes

Arrogance:

If there is one trait that can ensure your failure—regardless of your age, financial status, position or career—it is arrogance. Arrogance is often a camouflage for insecurity. People who are afraid to be real and vulnerable will often demonstrate this characteristic. Arrogance prevents growth, learning, the willingness to change, clarity of vision, peace, harmony in relationships, closeness with others and often happiness.

Why do people let this trait infiltrate their attitudes? Why don't they see its destructive patterns? Because we all have mental blocks—we fail to see clearly those characteristics sabotaging our success and happiness. Arrogance displays itself in some or all of the following behaviors (to mention a few):

- the unwillingness to see another's point of view
- the need to be right (first, best)
- the unwillingness to admit wrong
- the need to control people, events, circumstances
- poor listening skills

The key to eliminating this trait from your behavior is understanding and accepting that *who you are* is **not** *what you do* or *what you have.* It is not your roles, your position, your wealth, your fame or your power. It is the understanding that all of your talent and insights are God-given. Our role is to develop what we have been given, while realizing that without this divine guidance we are nothing. Oh, yes, you might live in a big home, drive an expensive car or run a successful business, but what value are any of these if you have lost the ability to be grateful and loving to those whom your life touches, or if you are filled with an empty longing?

Being arrogant, you might be successful, but I seriously doubt that you would have the ability to enjoy the rewards or have any sense of meaningful satisfaction.

"He who swells in prosperity will be sure to shrink in adversity."

Colton

Ego:

Everyone has an ego. It is the selfish part of us and it is necessary for survival. It can be useful in dealing with certain difficult situations or people. The problems begin when the ego gets out of hand and begins to consume attitudes, behavior and relationships.

Essentially, the ego wants us to:
1. control
2. manipulate
3. look good
4. look better than others
5. be perceived as smarter than others
6. talk about ourselves a great deal

When a person's ego is out of control, he/she can often be perceived by others as arrogant, aggressive, pushy, insensitive, manipulative and boring. It isn't that these people are boring, it is just that they want to dominate anything and everyone they interact with or touch. I am confident you know several people whose ego is out of control. I ask you, do you like being with them? Working for them? Being married to them? I'll bet not.

Why? Because they seem only to be interested in their own needs, desires, ideas and activities. They have little desire to listen to you or to your ideas—no matter how good your ideas may be. These people might even take credit for stolen ideas. What can you do if your ego is off the chart?

First of all, remember that you are not your ego unless

you choose to give up control of yourself to it. It is just one of the many parts of you. You are so much more than your ego. You are a spiritual being with a soul. You are a human being with a heart, which has the capacity to care, love, accept, understand and feel compassion. Secondly, don't forget that when your ego is in charge, your heart takes a back seat. Learn to take that 18-inch journey—living your life from your heart rather than your mind. Difficult, yes. Necessary for happiness, absolutely.

"Ambition without knowledge is ludicrous."

Tim Connor

Aging:

Welcome to the real world of getting old. There is a difference, however, between getting old and growing old. We all age – that's life – but none of us has to grow old. We can hold on to the outlook, spirit, and attitudes of our younger years and our youth. Youth is not a time, but a state of mind.

I know a great many people in their 20s and 30s who are old beyond their years, and I have also had the good fortune to know many people in their 80s and 90s with a youthful spirit and love of every moment.

Many people today are spending thousands of dollars to turn back the clock. Good luck! Can't be done. As one of life's senior citizens, I realize that I don't have the same energy, stamina or strength I did 30 or 40 years ago, but I do have the wisdom and understanding of all of those years due to mistakes in judgment and lessons learned.

There are many advantages to having been here for more than 50 or 60 years. I can hear some of you now, "Oh, yeah. What are they?" Well, you can get discounts at almost every business establishment in the country. You have the freedom of time now to do what you want rather than what you must. You have lots and lots of wonderful memories, and you may even have the joy of grandchildren.

As I look at my heroes, I can tell you that most of them didn't begin to make a difference or significant contribution until they hit their stride at 60, 70 or even 80. I think of people like Norman Vincent Peale, Bob Hope and Mother Theresa.

You have a choice – you can accept the aging process with dignity, style and grace, or you can fight every passing day begrudging every new wrinkle, ache and lost opportunity.

Why not put this time to good use? Share your wisdom, insight, and understanding with today's youth or the less fortunate. Why not give more back than you have taken from life?

"Everyone desires to live long, but no one would be old."

Swift

Poverty:

Poverty is not just about a lack of money or capital. There is poverty of the spirit and poverty of friends – and don't forget the poverty of love. When I speak of poverty, I am also referring to the opposite of abundance. There is no scarcity of stuff in the world. There is only a scarcity of belief, ideas, creativity, love, friendship and acceptance of others. Some people are rich who have little wealth, but are rich with the love of friends and family. Some people are poor who have more money than they could ever spend in a lifetime, but who are isolated, mistrusted and rule by fear and intimidation.

I read a wonderful illustration several years ago. It stated that, in a servant/master relationship, the power is in the hands of the servant. This person can choose to withhold his service to the master – so the master is always dependent on the servant. Remember the words of Jesus (I am an amateur on scripture so I will give you my interpretation): "Those of you who serve will rule in my Father's House." The paradox here is that those who rule really don't (rule), because they get their power from the many. If they didn't have any servants, what would they be master of? You guessed it: Nothing.

The teacher teaches, but he/she must have students. The manager manages, but must have employees. The parent directs, but must have children.

If you feel poor, why not take a few minutes and make a list of all of your blessings. Don't think you have any?

Well, let me get you started.

1 - you have air to breathe
2 - you have food to eat
4 - you have a body that works
5 - you have a mind that thinks
6 - you have water to drink
7 - *your turn...*

Make the list as long as you can, and then tell me you are poor.

"Love is like a beautiful flower which I may not touch, but whose fragrance makes the garden a place of delight just the same."

Helen Keller

Loss of a Loved One:

During my life, I have been one of the fortunate ones. I have only lost one person to death. Recently my mother passed away, and I can empathize with those of you who have known the sting of death.

There is this tremendous sense of loss. Memories that can never be shared again. Experiences you will never be able to tell them about. Laughter that is gone. Love that is gone. Friendship that is gone. Nothing but this emptiness in your heart.

When a loved one passes away – whether too soon as a young child, or later in the prime, or old as a grandparent who lived to the ripe old age of 95 – the hole in your heart is the same. We miss what could have been and will never be again.

Why does death hurt the living so much? Why do we grieve for our loved ones who have gone to a better place?

Our grieving is often selfishness. We feel cheated, left behind or alone. Why did they leave us? Why did they do this to us?

I cannot explain or rationalize the death of a young child because of a drunk driver or murderer running rampant through the halls of some high school or public place. I cannot understand why cancer takes the dear souls in our life, while drug pushers and financial scoundrels get off scotfree. I can only tell you that there must be a reason. It may be too difficult for me to comprehend with my limited spiritual wisdom, or it may be because I have not yet come to totally believe in God's master plan for salvation.

Regardless, feel your pain. Express your grief. Do not hide behind a fake smile. Send your departed loved ones your love and forgiveness. And then, move on. Yes, without them. I believe my mother will always be with me because she has a special place in my heart and my mind where she carved her name forever on the patchwork of my being. Our loved ones are not gone, just absent for a time. Keep the memory of them alive and active in your actions, decisions, beliefs and values.

"Death and love are the two wings that bear the good man to heaven."

M. Angelo

Fear:

Fear does strange things to many people. It causes them stress, anxiety, frustration, anger and uncertainty, and often immobilizes them against any action – rational or otherwise. Fear restricts blood flow, limits vision, raises blood pressure, and prevents clear thinking.

Fear, healthy fear, is a positive attribute in the right places and at the right times. It can prevent us from taking foolish and often life-threatening actions, and it can heighten our awareness that something is wrong or needs our attention. What is your typical reaction to those events, circumstances or people that bring fear into your consciousness? Do you run and hide? Confront it or them? Go into denial? Ignore it? Procrastinate on an action that will quickly eliminate the cause of your fear?

Years ago, I read a line that I have often forgotten when I needed it the most: "When you confront your fears, you will overcome them." When you ignore that of which you are afraid, it will haunt your mind, body and life like a relentless villain. What are you afraid of?

- The fear of success.
- The fear of failure.
- The fear of rejection.
- The fear of love.
- The fear of commitment.
- The fear of risk.
- The fear of the loss of love.
- The fear of death.
- The fear of being alone.

Fear can be a positive emotion. But, for most people, it stands between them and the fulfillment of their dreams. Refuse to let this character rule your life. Do something – anything. Take action. Do it now. Don't give fear a foothold in your life and your thoughts.

"Patience and time do more than strength or passion."

La Fontaine

Ignorance:

There is no excuse for ignorance in many parts of the world today – especially North America and Europe. There are over 90,000 books published every year in the United States alone. Almost every community has a library, and let's not forget the tremendous power of the Internet.

There are, however, different types of ignorance. There is:

- a lack of common sense
- a lack of emotional control
- a lack of common courtesies
- a lack of positive people skills
- a lack of effective communication ability

Why do many people insist on remaining ignorant? Why do people refuse to learn new skills, attitudes and abilities that could guarantee greater success and happiness? Don't have a clue, folks. I only know that, after over 30 years as a trainer and author, a very small percentage of people seriously want to learn. Oh yes, some give lip service to new ideas, new understanding and new wisdom, but few ever seem to integrate this information into their life.

And let's not forget that there is a difference between knowledge and wisdom. Knowledge is what you know or have learned. Wisdom is the ability to use what you have learned in the right way, at the right time, and with the appropriate people.

There are lots of college graduates working as waiters or waitresses. Now, I am belittling this profession. My point is that if you have a college degree or higher, what are you doing with it? I am not suggesting that everyone should aspire to a higher station in life. I am only wondering why, with this knowledge, some people refuse to use it more productively in their lives. Then there are the professional students. Those people who are afraid of responsibility and have chosen to make their life's work learning. To what end?

"As sure as ever God puts his children in the furnace, he will be in the furnace with them."

Spurgeon

Adversity:

To have a life without adversity is to live in Fantasyland. Sooner or later, adversity strikes its victims when they least expect it or want it. Adversity takes many forms. It can be:

- a business failure
- a broken relationship
- the loss of a job
- a financial crisis
- a health problem
- an automobile accident
- and hundreds and hundreds of other things

Adversity can bring people to their knees, or it can strengthen their resolve. It can turn an otherwise humble individual into a tiger, and it can cause the strongest souls to cringe in its wake. Why the difference?

Adversity is insensitive and neutral to its recipient's reactions or responses. It treats everyone the same. Each of us has the ability to reach down and grab the courage to overcome—a strength that we were not even aware we possessed. We can choose to overcome or we can choose to give in. The difference lies in a person's character, genes, history, commitment, will, and strength of desire. Adversity can be a patient teacher or it can be a tyrant. Again, the choice is ours.

As I look back over a life filled with adversity in every area, I can tell you from personal experience that I would not be who I am today had it not been for all of the challenges I have faced through the years. At the time, I resented them—each and every one of them. But today, in hindsight, they have given me the strength to carry on in the face of overwhelming odds. I don't know how my life will turn out, but I know one thing—I would not trade any of the adversity I have had to deal with for any amount of money.

"Courage consists not in hazarding without fear but being resolutely minded in a just cause."

Plutarch

Self-Acceptance:

Many people are searching for acceptance outside of themselves when they haven't yet learned to accept themselves. Self-acceptance is being O.K. with who you are, how you got here, and where you are going. It is patience with and loving yourself even when you make mistakes, fail, or do really stupid things.

Self-acceptance is a close relative of self-esteem. It is difficult to have one without the other, and, if you have one, you will tend to have the other. Why do people have low self-acceptance? There are many reasons, but most fall into the following categories:

1- The need to be perfect. 2- The need to be right. 3- The need for approval and to be liked. 4- Feeling inadequate due to some perceived lack of ability or skill. 5- Staying stuck in mistakes and errors of judgment in the past. 6- An extraordinary concern for other people's opinions and views about you. 7- A focus on your imperfections rather than your blessings. 8- A strong need to please others. 9- An ego that is out of control. 10- Emotional immaturity.

To accept yourself fully is to recognize that you will never be perfect. You are not finished making mistakes. You will fail again. Not everyone you meet will like you. A happy and contented life is not about what happens and why, but what you do with it or about it. Very few people will agree with you on numerous occasions. And you will die with some unfinished business. The key to gaining self-acceptance is to recognize that you are in process as a human being and, as a result of that process, your growth comes when you need it most.

Your job is to take yourself lightly and what you do seriously.

It only means that you do the best you can with what you have at the time, and let the stuff that is not within your control go – either emotionally, physically or psychologically.

"Sit loosely in the saddle of life."

Robert Louis Stevenson

Pride:

Pride can be good, but pride can destroy a person in a heartbeat.

What is it about pride that steals from a person's self-worth, vulnerability and humility? I am reminded of the words of one of my favorite authors, John Powell. In his book *Why Am I Afraid to Tell You Who I Am?*, John spends a great deal of time talking about being real. Why are people afraid to let down their guard and show the world their true self, insecurity and pain? Is it out of fear? Is it out of uncertainty? Or is it just a protective device people use to shield themselves from the hurts, slights and unkind words and deeds of others?

Pride is also a worthy attribute when you have done a deed well, overcome an obstacle or won the day. An athlete has the right to feel good about a victory. A salesperson has the right to feel good in making the biggest sale of their career. A mother has the right to feel pride in a child who has turned out to be a model citizen and exceptional person. But then, there is false pride – the feeling of a sense of satisfaction or smugness when, in reality, there is no right to the emotion. This is used only as a crutch to get through the maze of human issues that confront us all.

I can remember, over ten years ago, earning an award in the speaking profession after more than 15 years of effort, persistence and commitment. I can recall the feeling of being on stage in front of 1,500 of my peers. My heart was filled with a sense of pride. As I have looked back at that event, I now see that my pride was misplaced. Oh, yes, I deserved it – I earned it. But the real gratitude must go to the hundreds of clients who had confidence in me, the thousands of audience members who trusted me and the dozens of friends and peers who encouraged me in times of doubt.

We do nothing on our own. The glory of our works should be given to the One who gives us the tools. That, my friends, is your God.

"There is nothing more awful than conscious humility, it is the most Satanic type of pride."

Chambers

Addiction:

There are many types of addiction. People can be addicted to love, alcohol, drugs, sex, food, money, stimulants, power, fame – to name a few. There are certain common reasons for addiction, regardless of which it may be, and other causes of addiction may be unique. Let's look at some of the common ones first.

- a desire for excess
- a lack of self-control
- a lack of self-love
- low self-esteem

Some of the unique causes are:

- excess ambition
- insecurity
- uncontrolled ego gratification
- the need to manipulate
- a desire to punish others
- self-hate

I don't want to get into a tit-for-tat with any professional health care counselors over this. I feel that addiction causes a great deal of pain and suffering—not only for many of the participants, but also for family, friends and co-workers.

Addictions, whether kept hidden from others or openly flaunted, contribute to divorce, abuse, abandonment, suicide, automobile accidents, transfer of unhealthy diseases, physical suffering, premature death, loneliness, discomfort and any number of other negative outcomes. If this is true, then why do people persist in continuing their addictions? If I had an answer to that, friends, I'd be on my yacht in the Caribbean rather than sitting at my computer writing.

"Peace rules the day, where reason rules the mind."

Collins

Poor Health:

You've heard, "If you have your health, you have every-thing." Well, I know some very influential and success-ful people who have had constant health challenges. Yes, health is important, but not having it is not an excuse to refuse to do something positive with your life.

I have nothing but the greatest compassion for people who have had health challenges in the past, or are facing them today. But, having said that, I also know that many people use poor health as a reason for doing little with their lives.

Health is a gift and disease is the absence of health. It is not the absence of courage, faith, will, belief and com-mitment. It is difficult to carry on when every move-ment is painful or every breath a struggle, but think for a moment why you were given poor health. Was it to be a beacon for others? Was it to demonstrate that courage, faith and belief can overcome?

There are numerous examples and case studies of peo-ple who had every reason to die due to health circum-stances, and yet they lived. There are also many illustra-tions of people in good health who, for no other reason than the loss of the will to live, died.

My father is one of my favorite examples. Over ten years ago, he was given just a few years to live due to cancer. Fortunately, he chose not to accept this fate due to the responsibility of caring for his wife. Today he has more health challenges than any ten people, yet he will celebrate his 86th birthday next month. As a postscript, he has outlived many of his physicians.

I also think of Christopher Reeve, one of my heroes. If you know his story, you know that it would have been easy for him to give up, paralyzed from the neck down due to an accident. But he has chosen not only to survive, but also to make a difference. Everyone may not have his resolve and will, but they can at least strive for it in themselves.

"Truth is a glorious but hard mistress. She never consults, bargains or compromises."

A. W Tozer

Failure:

Some people will go to any length to avoid failure. Please understand from the onset that I am not advocating failure for failure's sake. I am, however, going to suggest that without failure it is very difficult, if not impossible, to accomplish great things. That may sound like a strange paradox, but most of life is—so why shouldn't the concepts of failure and success be included?

Show me someone who has never failed at anything, and I will show you someone who always plays it safe, never stretches, and is willing to accept the status quo, whatever that means to them. Show me someone who has succeeded at anything, and I will show you someone who goes for the gold, shoots for the stars and is willing to pick himself up off the floor again and again until he has achieved his dreams. Dreams can change, goals can change, circumstances can change, conditions can change. But the inner drive to overcome, accomplish, win, contribute or feel the glow of personal satisfaction can never be dampened in those who have come to this life believing they are here to win at something or everything.

They understand that to overcome, they will have to go around, dig under or fly over—but the obstacles are there to test their resolve and commitment and not to stop them. These people understand that they might not make it over the first time or the second or even the tenth, but as long as they have the health required (and there are many people who have even overcome these personal challenges), they will win the day.

These people use their failures as assignments in the classroom of life. They see these setbacks as requirements to learn how to do it better, faster, slower, sooner, later... whatever. How about you? Ever failed? If so, what was your reaction or response to it? Failing at something now? How are you feeling? What are you doing about it? What are you learning? How are you responding? Or are you the type who always plays it safe?

"Any officer who is afraid of failure will never win! Any man who is afraid to die will never really live."

Gen. Patton

Uncertainty:

Many people today struggle with the need to know what will happen tomorrow, next week or this year. Some have the need to manipulate tomorrow or to have life be 'in order' or 'certain.'

I never thought my life would turn out this way. How about you? Is your life unfolding exactly the way you want? Planned? Expected? I doubt it. It is probably either turning out better than you thought, or, in some ways, worse. Life is about uncertainty, adventure, unknowns and surprises. Yes, some of these surprises can be positive, while some can be negative (remember that everyone defines positive and negative by their own perceptions, experiences and parameters). What are some of the uncertainties in life? I don't really need to tell you because I am confident you have experienced some—but here are a few anyway:

- a career change you didn't anticipate.
- a divorce you never thought possible.
- a health crisis you were not prepared for.
- a new relationship at the wrong time in your life.
- a financial challenge you felt you did not deserve.
- a family problem with children, in-laws, siblings.

There are many others, but for most people they seem to fall within the above list. There are two ways to live life: release the struggle to know in advance what your life may bring, or fight life and all of its uncertainty by trying to create a known outcome.

I can only tell you that sooner or later in every life there will be unknowns. That's life, folks. The key is to have a working philosophy or life outlook that enables you to get through all of these challenges, adventures and surprises with dignity, peace, balance and inner harmony. These so-called surprises, in the end, can be a wonderful detour through life.

"Patience and fortitude conquer all things."

Emerson

Difficult People:

Ever had to deal with a difficult person? A boss, spouse, child, customer, teacher or friend? They are everywhere and they are not just filling the prisons in this country. What exactly is a difficult person? Two of the most common issues troubling us concerning other people and their behaviors are: 1) people see life differently, and 2) the issue of faults. No one looks at life—its events, conditions or circumstances—the sameway. We see life not as it is, but as we are. Each of us has a mental filter through which we interpret other people's behavior, events and circumstances. Ten people can look at the same piece of art, auto accident, movie or sunset and see it differently. This gives life its diversity and its relationships their challenges.

One example I use in my seminar on relationships for couples is the idea of faults. Do you know of someone who has faults? Be honest, now. Look closely at him for a moment. Aren't another person's faults what that person thinks, feels, believes or does differently than what you think he should feel, think, believe or act? The assumption you are making when assuming another person has a fault is that your way of feeling, acting, etc. is either better than his or right. Now isn't that ridiculous?

There is no right or wrong, only difference. This is one of the major issues causing stress and conflict within personal relationships. The need to change the other person to your way of thinking because his is wrong and yours is right… Acceptance of differences is perhaps the biggest hurdle people face in relationships.

Truth IS. It is not our interpretation of it, and yet so many people believe that their truth should be everyone's truth. Where are your perceptions about life, people, events, circumstances, the past, present or future clouded? Where do you need a clearer vision and more accurate perceptual integrity?

"There is no better way to keep God out of your soul than to be full of self."

Fulton Sheen

Lack of Direction:

Everyone is where he or she is supposed to be and doing what he or she is supposed to be doing. Now I know some of you might disagree with this premise. I, too, have had my doubts over the years. This doesn't mean that you won't be somewhere else tomorrow, doing something different next week and with someone new next year. The principle also is not designed to give people permission to change something—anything—just for the sake of changing it—on a whim.

Each of us is on a path through life that has many curves, hills, detours, great views, accidents, time spent lost and alone, peaks, valleys, accomplishments and failures. Life is not about trying to manipulate the Universe into giving you what you believe you want or is in your best interest. It is about learning to flow with what crosses your path whether positive or negative. It is not about giving in, but trusting the process of your life and the decisions you make along the way.

It is unfortunate that many people want to have their life in nice neat pre-determined packages with predictable outcomes. This would be lovely if it were true, even possible. Life is not about the future or the past. It is about learning to do the best you can where you are with what you have. This doesn't mean you won't know more next week, have more next month, or be better next year.

Life is not about where you end up, but the roads or direction you travel. Some of us, and I include myself in this group, have spent a lot of time searching and lost.

Some of us have abandoned the search, while others don't give a rip about creating a better life through increased wisdom and practical experience. I am a romantic at heart. I believe that if we do our part and trust God and life, we will one day smell the flowers of love, feel the warm caress of success and experience inner joy and peace as we travel into our own personal sunset – regardless of what age we might be.

So many people live with unfulfilled dreams, broken hearts, loneliness, fear and emptiness. It doesn't have to be that way. The way to change your future, and therefore your memories, is to travel in the right direction today in those areas of your life that are important to you.

I leave you with 3 simple questions:

1. Who are you becoming, and are you comfortable with him or her?
2. Do you live each day with gratitude for the gift of life you have been given that day?
3. Are you at peace with your journey, or are you in a relentless chase for something else, something less, or something more tomorrow?

"There is no prosperity without adversity."

Welsh Saying

Spiritual Emptiness:

Our spirit lives in a positive environment, regardless of our human attempts to sabotage it. Each of us, whether we choose to accept it or not, or believe it or not, is a spiritual being. We were given the gift of life by God and our parents. This life, your life, has a purpose and a reason for its existence. Much of your searching as you travel your life's path is to discover this purpose.

When people, for whatever reason, lose this sense of connection to their Creator, they often find themselves lost and leading a life without meaning. Each of us is here to make a difference. We are here to fulfill God's purpose in this world. If you have not found what you believe is your destiny, is it possible that you are trying to manipulate God into giving you a destiny you want rather than what He wants for you?

Many people feel that someone, everyone, is better off than they are or more successful than they are. They covet someone else's success, gifts, fame, power or influence. I know. I did. Years ago, I had a goal to be the number one motivational speaker in the world. It wasn't until I had been brought to my knees on several occasions that I finally accepted the fact that this was not in store for me. It was to be the best Tim Connor I was capable of becoming, and to spend more of my time writing than speaking.

I fought this destiny with every fiber of my being for a number of years until I saw the light (not literally, folks) and began to spend more time writing than speaking.

Well, friends, lessons are often short-lived. I then decided that I wanted to be the number one writer in the country of self-help literature (I guess the light I saw wasn't bright enough). I was missing a fundamental truth in life – that God makes the plans and I execute them – whatever they are. And my purpose is to do it with love and gratitude. So, you are reading my 31st book. Hope you are enjoying it!

"This world is the land of the dying: the next is the land of the living."

Tryon Edwards

Emotional Immaturity:

By emotional immaturity, I am referring to the inability to positively control emotions such as fear, anger, guilt, jealousy, envy, pride.

Some people spend their lives on autopilot. They permit others to push their buttons, and therefore turn the power of their own emotions over to the other person. I can recall a time when I had a disagreement with a friend whom I felt had wronged me, and I carried around a great deal of anger for weeks. I never saw this person again, but gave him permission to control my feelings and emotional reactions. Strange thing was I didn't even like him anymore. Doesn't make much sense does it? Well, it didn't to me either. I decided from that point on that I was going to be in charge of my emotions, reactions and feelings.

Once I gave up the ability of others to manipulate me in this way, a number of things happened.

- I started to like myself better.
- I began to feel more in control.
- I stopped worrying about what others thought about me.
- I was happier.
- I made more money.
- I had more 'real' friends.

I suggest you keep one thing in mind as you interact with others. If you want to get better control of any negative emotional reactions, accept that you have a right to feel the way you feel as long as it doesn't negatively impact those around you. But remember that you can't afford the luxury of letting others make you feel how they would like you to feel—because they then believe they have power over you. My friend in the above example didn't even know I was experiencing all of this anger. I was, however, and this anger wasn't hurting him at all, it was only hurting me.

"The price of greatness is responsibility."

Churchill

Success:

What is success for you? Even more importantly, when will you know you have achieved it? These are two critical questions that we must have reasonable insight into as we move toward our destinies in life.

As I have traveled around the world for the past twenty years giving speeches and seminars on a variety of topics, I have noticed a very intriguing philosophy that many people use as their benchmark for success.

Most people in life see their success as grounded in some future event, relationship or set of circumstances—or in the past, with all of its achievement and history. Future dreams and desires or past accomplishments. Future plans or past accolades. Future projects or past gains. Future relationships or past lessons learned.

I, too, have been guilty many times in my life of deluding myself that I had arrived or would soon arrive at some mystical point or place in the future. I saw success as an unknown or vague uncertainty depending on the whims of management decisions, corporate outcomes, relationship activities or the persistent, yet relentless, passage of time. I moved through life's mistakes, failures and opportunities, pulled into life's hopes, dreams and fantasies toward new horizons.

My activities in the present—writing this book, for example—always had to have some specific connection to some "outcome." These future frozen moments in time represented the timeline of my life. A series of wins and losses registered on the calendar of the universe. Three vital questions that people continually ask themselves are: "What is my Destiny in life?" "How will I achieve it, and when will I know if I am on the right road?" Success is not in your future. It is not an accumulation of past accomplishments. People smarter than I have been defining success for centuries. If you didn't like one person's definition, there was always another that you could use as your guiding philosophy through life. Success, for many, is an illusive, transitory process, leaving behind empty memories, void of their purpose and value when lived.

For these people, success is in the eye of the beholder. It depends on other's acceptance, recognition and praise. They are in a race to prove their value and worth to the world. Even though I used many of these "outside in" definitions for years as my platform for success, I was often left with the haunting feeling that there was still something missing in my life. It was only in the past few years that I began to think rather than memorize. Success is, to me, not the illusion of fleeting daily successful activities, decisions and projects, but the ability to relish the joy, the sense of gratitude and opportunity, to be able to live "inside out" rather than "outside in."

"If you are not ready today, you will be even less so tomorrow."

Ovid

Forgiveness:

One of the most difficult things for people to do is to forgive others for their mistakes, transgressions or errors in judgment.

Forgiveness is not about letting the other person off the hook for his behavior. Forgiveness doesn't say, "What you did was OK or acceptable." Forgiveness is about letting *yourself* off the emotional hook. It is about releasing its negative hold on your emotions, feelings or attitudes.

The value of forgiveness is for you, not necessarily the other person. For example, let's say your parents did something to you years ago, and you have not been able to forgive them for some reason. Let's also say that they have passed on to the next world. How can you forgive them? Isn't it too late? Yes, it is too late to tell them you forgive them. They have died. But it is not too late to send forgiveness to them, thereby releasing the grief, pain or anxiety that holding on to this lack of forgiveness causes you.

Why is it so hard for people to forgive? Do we really need to hold on to any unforgiveness about anything anyone has ever done or said to us? When we believe someone needs our forgiveness, we are assuming that they did something to hurt or disappoint us, or cause us pain of some kind.

Everyone is just doing the best they can to get through this life with as little stress, heartache, and trouble as they can. When someone hurts us or causes us pain, is it because we had too high of an expectation of him? Is this issue really ours and not his? One of the greatest causes of disappointment is the unrealized expectation of another person's behavior.

Sooner or later, everyone you know will disappoint you in some way. It is inevitable. Does this mean that we will always need to forgive others? Or, would a better approach be to understand that these people did not mean to hurt us? Most people are not setting out to give us grief.

Yes, I will agree that there are people who have made it their life's purpose to hurt, invalidate, and in some way wreck havoc in other's lives.

To see yourself as a victim is to wish your circumstances to continue.

Who do you need to forgive and why? Remember, forgiveness is not about the other person. It is about who you are and who you are becoming.

"Kindness is the golden chain by which society is bound together."

Goethe

Loss of a Job or Business:

I can recall over thirty years ago when I was fired from my first sales position. I had two children with another one on the way and not a spare dime to my name. I can remember as if it were yesterday the overwhelming sense of desperation I felt. I was letting my family down; I was even letting myself down. I didn't know what to do or where to turn. I only knew I needed a job and I needed one NOW.

Several years after that, I also lost a business. The story and the gory details are too long to go into—suffice it to say, I once again felt this tremendous sense of despair. Everything I had worked so hard for was gone in less than a week.

What defines you? Your success? Your position? Your power or fame? Is it who you know or play golf with?

It's just a job, folks—nothing more. You got that one; you can get another one. Now, I am not an advocate of jumping from one ship to the next every six months or every time your boss or company does something you dislike. But few people today stay at the same job or career their entire life. If you have, I salute you. If you haven't, I would ask you why you left.

Jobs are about work, not fun. We don't tell our friends that we can't stay out late partying because we have to go to 'fun' tomorrow. We work so we can create lifestyle —so we can have fun, travel, spend, etc.

If you find yourself out of work, see it as an opportunity to improve yourself, your life, your lifestyle or your relationship with someone. See it as an opportunity to get into another position or career that is more consistent with your goals, needs, desires or philosophy.

Whining won't help. Complaining won't help. Blaming others won't help. Feeling sorry for yourself won't help. Giving up won't help. Got it? Now go for it.

"Great works are performed not by strength but by perseverance."

Johnson

Greed:

I have a lot of opinions that I usually keep to myself, but I am going to make an exception with this topic.

I believe that the major cause of all crime, heartache, failure and unrest in the world today is greed.

What would happen to the millions of jobs and profits in the healthcare system if no one ever got sick? What would happen to the millions of jobs in all of the jails, courts, and law offices if there were no more crime? Need I go on?

Greed drives many businesses today. Greed is the cause of the drug problem in the world today. Greed is the cause of political unrest in countries around the globe.

Greed keeps employers from sharing with their employees. It prevents customers from being honest about causes of mistakes, and it is indirectly creating a wedge between generations.

People want more, bigger, faster, better, and then they want to start all over again. Fortunately, there are many people in the world who are generous with their time, talent and money. They fund the hundreds of charities, churches, education programs, and sponsor-paid media.

I salute you, each and every one of you, for your generosity and compassion. I especially salute those of you with truly noble reasons for your giving.

The less fortunate in our world need help. Be thankful you are not one of them. You don't go to bed hungry every night. You don't have to drink polluted water and you have the most important human emotion in your pocket—hope.

"He is a wise man who does not grieve for the things which he has not but rejoices for those which he has."

Epictetus

Financial Crisis:

I could write an entire book about this topic. I have been broke three times in my life, and I can tell you, the view from the bottom of the pile is not very good. Everything in our lives is there to help us to learn a valuable lesson. When we fail to learn this lesson, unfortunately we get another opportunity to learn it. And another, and another... if we persist in failing to pay attention to our life teachers.

Money is a tool—nothing more—that creative people use for any number of reasons—some worthy and some not so worthy. Money, unfortunately, is the primary measuring stick used today by most people to determine their worth as a person. I have known a lot of wealthy jerks, and I have also had the honor to know many hard-working, decent people who were good friends, parents, spouses and sons or daughters, squeaking by financially week after week, year after year.

You are not your money and your money is not you, and I don't really care what you are doing with it. I have met some very wealthy people who gave a great deal to charity only for the recognition, and I know people who have very little and give a great deal (more than they can afford) to others.

Financial crises are valuable tools. They can teach you humility, tolerance, creativity, a valuable work ethic, caution, and any number of worthwhile lessons.

So, if you are in the middle of a crisis, don't whine,

blame or feel sorry for yourself—get busy. If you are wealthy and want for nothing, don't get too cocky—you never know. And besides, no one can buy his way into God's good graces. Trust me, He doesn't need your cash or your gifts of charity. He is doing very well, thank you, on His own. Remember that money is a measuring stick for your success and worth, but only if that is how you choose to be measured.

"To reach the port of Heaven we must sail sometimes with the wind and sometimes against it. But we must sail and not drift nor lie at anchor."

O.W. Holmes

Low Self-Esteem:

Low self-esteem is one of the biggest causes of many of today's ills—both in relationships and in society. This issue is at the root of much addiction, abuse, crime, health problems and business or career failures. Why, you ask? How we feel about ourselves is something we bring into every relationship, business transaction, marriage, and activity or project. Whether you like yourself or feel you need to change something about yourself to be acceptable or even lovable to others is a curse many people deal with every day.

When you have difficulty accepting or liking yourself or feeling accepted or liked by others for who you are, you will feel the need to take actions that win you the acceptance or love you desire and crave. People choose to take drugs, dress a particular way, have cosmetic surgery, drink, smoke, take careers, read certain books, attend various churches and diet all in the name of belonging.

I can recall in a previous relationship that I felt like a worm. My self-esteem hit bottom because I no longer felt valuable. What I didn't realize was that I was more concerned about the acceptance and validation by my spouse than with self-acceptance of who I was and who I was becoming. It has taken years, but I have learned that whether you like and accept me has nothing to do with me, but has everything to do with you and your beliefs, values, expectations, opinions, prejudices and judgments. When you judge me, you are only defining yourself.

There is only one way to learn to like, love and accept yourself, and that is to understand that your value is not about what you achieve, accomplish, own, learn or share. It is only about the realization that, in the sight of God, you are a precious being. He doesn't need you to look younger, have blonde hair, be thinner or smarter. He only asks that you love his child (you) as he does—unconditionally. Yes, if you are thinner, you might live longer; and yes, if you are smarter, you might get a promotion or a better job. But, 100 years from now, none of that will matter.

"We are always in the forge, or on the anvil; by trials God is shaping us for higher things."

H. W. Beecher

Expectations:

One of the biggest causes of disappointment and frustration in life is unmanaged expectations. By this, I am not implying that you should not shoot for the moon. Positive thinking is better than negative thinking. Being optimistic is better than being pessimistic. However, keep in mind that there may be factors beyond your control having an impact on your destiny, success and goal achievement.

What if the company drops a product line, and it was your best seller? What if a new recruit promises to jump out of the gate full force, and then never makes the first call? The list is endless. Here are a few keys to consider when managing your expectations to ensure you don't live with disappointment, and also don't sabotage your opportunity with negative thinking.

Ask yourself:

1. Do I have total control over this outcome?
2. Has this person/situation ever disappointed me before?
3. What were the conditions?
4. How do I respond to disappointment?
5. How do I feel about people who break promises?
6. Am I ever guilty of not doing what I said I would do?
7. Do I tend to take people's commitments lightly or seriously?
8. Do I trust people who tend to let me down?
9. Do I tend to hold people accountable for their promises?

10. Am I often disappointed?

One of the biggest causes of stress is the expectation of another person's behavior. Why won't my kids, spouse, friends, etc. behave the way I would or I think they should? They never will. They are not you. Sooner or later, everyone will disappoint you. Not being pessimistic here, folks, just a realist.

"If I fail, it will be for lack of ability and not of purpose."

Lincoln

Perfection:

I once had an assistant who was a perfectionist. She taught me that people who want or need to be perfect lack a fundamental understanding of life. Nothing is perfect. Everything just is. Nature is not perfect, life is not perfect, businesses are not perfect and relationships are not perfect. None of these ever will be. Only God is perfect in His love, grace and unconditional acceptance. Everything else has flaws.

Now please, don't misunderstand me. I don't want typos in this book, but I guarontee, if you look hard and long enough, you will find some. Does that make this book less valuable because I misspelled guarantee in the previous sentence? (Did it on purpose if you haven't figured that out yet). If it does, then you are missing the point. Perfection is not about perfect, but the willingness to try and be better, stronger, wiser or kinder, or whatever.

Often, perfectionists have low self-esteem. They have a fundamental need to be good so others can perceive them as good. We are not good because of what we do, but because of who we are. Just because I write a book with a few mistakes in it, does that make me less of a person? Sure, you say, I should learn to spell or type better or find a better editor. Trust me, there are no perfect editors either.

Perfection is defined by Webster as (I hate dictionary definitions but, in this case, I will make an exception and share it with you): "A personal standard, attitude or philosophy that demands perfection—excellence—and rejects anything less." This doesn't leave much hope for most of us.

Think about something for a moment if you would. If you were perfect in anything, what would you have left to work for, strive for or live for? Yes, getting better is better than getting worse, but if I had to choose between a) being perfect, and b) being happy and feeling a sense of self-satisfaction in spite of my imperfections—I'd take happy every time. There is a great old saying: "Would you rather be happy or right?"

"Don't be so humble, you're not that good."

Golda Meir

Lack of Motivation:

Sooner or later everyone loses his motivation, ambition or sense of urgency about life, career, relationships or business. These times come when we have temporarily lost our sense of purpose or goal-direction. It is not a time to whine or feel sorry for yourself. It should be a time of reflection and self-evaluation.

I have known this sense of loss, of 'why continue on in the face of certain disaster or failure.' I can recall reading my one-thousandth rejection letter from a publisher. I thought to myself, "Why bother struggling over this computer at 25 words per minute to write another book that no one will buy or read? Why not just go work in my garden?"

I have known many people who have sold businesses when, at the ripe old age of 45, they lost their motivation. I have known people who have struggled all their lives for just one quick glimpse of success or happiness. I have also known many people who struggled against every conceivable odd, and have persevered. They may not have hit a home run, or become a millionaire, but they certainly can sit back and pat themselves on the back for a worthwhile life.

So, I can hear your wheels turning. What's the point of struggling all your life toward a goal and never reaching it? One thing I have learned in life is that life is not in the achievement, but in the trip.

People who lose their motivation (or never had it to

begin with) suffer from a sense of lack of control over their own destinies. They have this attitude that they are not responsible for the outcomes in their lives—that they deserve to have, be, learn, earn whatever without paying the price. I can only tell you that it is not that kind of world. There is a price-reward ratio that we all must live by. If you want the rewards, however you define them, then you must pay the price. Fail to pay the price and life says, "you don't get the prize."

Anyone who lacks motivation is doomed to live a life of mediocrity, boredom or sameness.

"We have to work out what God works in, and the way we work it out is by the mechanical process of habit."

Chambers

Surrender:

One of my biggest challenges in life has been the willingness and ability to surrender. A phrase that I often read is: "Once you accept something and surrender, the struggle ends." Permit me to share a brief personal example.

I have been writing books for over twenty years. During that same time, I have received over 1,000 rejection letters from publishers. Last summer, I finally surrendered and decided to stop sending books to publishers for consideration. Within a week, I received two calls from two different publishers wanting me to write books for them. I asked myself "Why now?" Was this just the result of thousands of hours of self-promotion? Would these calls have come without my surrender? I can't answer that. I can only tell you that, once I surrendered, there was a tremendous sense of relief.

Why can't people surrender? What prevents them from letting go and trusting God? Why do they feel they need to be in control at all times? I believe it is for one of the following reasons:

- fear that, if they surrender, they won't get what they want.
- a lack of trust that, when whatever does come (even though it wasn't what they wanted), it is in their best interests.
- a philosophy of life that says, "I can do this, I don't need help."
- fear that they won't get what they think they need.

- arrogance that they know better than anyone what is best for them.

Letting go is not easy. It is like changing a bad habit. You try, but then you fall back again and again into the same old habit patterns.

There is only one way to surrender for good, and that is to learn to trust God for everything in your life. This doesn't mean you can sit home and wait for your success; you have to do the work. The Quakers have a saying: "Pray, but move your feet."

"Knowledge and timber should not be much used until they are seasoned."

O.W. Holmes

Struggle:

Why is struggle a part of life? Any time you try any-
thing difficult or new, you are bound to have some type
of struggle. Exercise requires struggle. Changing an
opinion, belief, expectation or attitude requires struggle.
Any time you attempt growth in any area of your life,
you will struggle. Why is it, then, that some people seem
to go through life with no apparent struggle, while oth-
ers seem to attract it into their life with every breath? I
have known struggle in every area of my life: my career,
my relationships, my financial life and my willingness
to let go and surrender.

Struggle is not in our genes, but in our minds and in our
reactions to life. It is not in our environment, but in our
expectations. It is not in the circumstances or people in
our lives, but in our desires.

The problem here is that each of us is trying to develop,
design and live our ideal life, but we don't know what it
will or should look like. We are trying to move into a
happy and successful future, but we don't seem to know
how to create it. We all want something more, better or
less, in some area of our life, but are at a loss as to why
we don't or can't have it.

Struggle is not necessary in our life. It is not required.
Please note—I am not including the following in any
definition of struggle: effort, failure, problems, risks,
losses, broken dreams, lost loves, disappointment,
stress, etc.

Struggle is our reaction to life: its successes, frustrations, achievements, failures and challenges. The level of struggle for each of us is defined by each of us in our own way using our own yardstick. I have spent many hours contemplating why I have often lived a life of struggle. My answer is: I wanted it and needed it to move me forward. Seems like a strange attitude I know, but it is the best I have come up with so far. Maybe when my life is struggle-free, I will have a better answer, but until then I seem to be cursed with this need to fight life every step of the way. I am discovering that when I release my attachments—the struggle ends.

How about you? What are you struggling with today? In this life? In your career or business? Your relationships? Once you let it go and surrender, the struggle seems to end. Try it, it might work for you, too. And you just might be happier and more successful in the process!

"The difficulty in life is choice."

George Moore

Worry:

I recently came across an interesting statistic. Now generally, statistics can be very misleading, but they can give us some insight if we don't get ourselves worked into a twit over them. Anyway, I read that 85 - 90% of the population worry about something on a consistent basis. People worry about:

- their health
- their career or job
- their finances
- their future
- their kids/relatives
- their life in general
- what other people think of them
- and anything else they can think of.

Worry was depicted in ancient hieroglyphics with a picture of a wolf sinking his teeth into the neck of a man. In other words, worry literally cuts off the flow of life from the brain to the body and from the body back to the brain. I have also read, years ago, that a large percentage of what people worry about never comes to pass. In other words, worry is a down payment on a debt you will never owe. So, why do people worry?

1. They believe they have no control over their life and its outcomes.
2. They tend to be pessimistic and negative.
3. They feel they are victims, and that life is picking on them and is out to get them.
4. They don't believe they have any positive options for

events or circumstances.
5. They tend to live either in the future or in the past.

What good does worry do us? None. If this is so, why do people insist on giving so much mental energy to an activity that could be better directed to some other, more productive objective like a hobby, a general interest, a creative endeavor, time with loved ones, time for reading or entertainment, time for activity or exercise?

Here are a few things you can do if you are a worrier:

1. Keep a worry list. Every time you start to worry about something, write it down and see how often it comes to pass. But get it out of your mind and onto the paper.
2. Learn to live in the present moment, rather than in the future.
3. Focus on what you can do, not what you can't.
4. See worry for what it is: useless mental energy that could be better used elsewhere.
5. Learn to keep things in perspective: nothing going on in your life right now will matter much in a hundred years.

"First say to yourself what you would be; then do what you have to do."

Epictetus

Change:

I have recently taken up whitewater rafting as a new hobby. This is my third year experiencing the thrill, as well as the self-discovery, this activity can provide. Recently I spent the day on a river in Tennessee that was used for training whitewater Olympians.

During the first Class 5 rapid, someone threw me out of the raft. I know I didn't just fall out on my own! I spent the next 60 seconds on my back in one of the wildest rides I have ever experienced. I careened from one ragged boulder to another while gasping for air, hoping that it would all end soon. My life passed in front of me several times while the water kept trying to own me. If you have never done a Class 5 rapid, filled with rocks, on your back, I don't advise it. When I was finally able to grasp the rope that was thrown to me by another rafter, I understood the lessons of this mishap—kind of like life.

1. Enjoy the ride.
2. Trust in the outcome.
3. Recognize that there will be times of uncertainty.
4. Keep things in perspective.
5. Change is the word of the day.
6. You can't change the river. It will go where it wants.
7. Be grateful for small things, even a rope at the right time.
8. Never underestimate your seatmate on a raft.
9. Trust those you don't know, especially if they are in another raft.
10. Rocks are good. They create the rapids. They con-

tribute to the adventure.
11. You have to start the trip to enjoy the ride.
12. Rapids eventually end and the water becomes still and quiet.

Enjoy the adventure of life today. Today is a gift. Be thankful and give to this day and take from it all that you can and all that you are.

"Cease to inquire what the future has in store, and take as a gift whatever the day brings forth."

Horace

Problems:

One of my heroes, the late Norman Vincent Peale, once said, "There is only one group of people that don't have problems, and they are all dead. Problems are a sign of life. So the more problems you have, the more alive you are." My addition to Norman's quote would be, "If you don't have any problems today, maybe you are on the way out of here and you don't know it yet."

This can be perceived as a tongue-in-cheek philosophy of life; however, it is closer to the truth than you might think. One thing you and I have both learned is that everyone has problems. Some have relationship problems, others financial, some career, others health, some social, others business. No one is immune to problems in life.

The key is to accept the issues, negatives, problems, situations (I don't care what you call them) as a part of the life process of becoming. Failures, whiners or victims see problems as life 'picking' on them.

Winners, regardless of their position, status, age or circumstances, see problems and adversity as catalysts to becoming better, stronger, wiser, and more aware of the reality of their lives.

Problems are not positive or negative; they are neutral. It isn't what is happening in your life that matters; it is how you choose to see it and what you do with it.

Learn to see the negatives as loving teachers in your life

—bringing you the opportunity to get a clearer vision of where you need attitude adjustments, improved thinking or better skills.

"It better befits a man to laugh at life rather than to lament over it."

Seneca

Stress:

Stress in life is normal. Everything causes stress. There are positive stressors such as promotions, marriage, relocation, starting a business, winning the lottery, retirement, having a baby. There are also negative stressors such as failure, getting fired, divorce, missing a deadline, having a baby, getting promoted, starting a business, winning the lottery, death of a loved one, relocating, etc., etc., etc.

Did you notice that I repeated some of the items in each list? Not a mistake, folks. It was intentional. Stress is not about what is happening, but about how you respond to those things (I just summarized my full day seminar on managing stress in your life).

Stressors are not positive or negative. A relocation can be positive for one person and negative for another. A promotion can do the same, and so can all of the others I mentioned, as well as all of the ones I didn't. Wait a minute, Tim. How can the death of a loved one be interpreted as a positive stressor? Personally, I don't know of anyone who wishes for the death of a loved one. But, I am confident that somewhere in this world there is someone who will be relieved when a sick relative finally passes away, no longer having to deal with the pain and humiliation that disease can cause.

Stress is not caused by events. If it were, everyone would have the same reaction or response to similar events, and we know that this isn't true. Stress can kill you or keep you alive. Stress can and will destroy your happiness if you do not learn to accept the reality of life, and all of its issues, stuff, problems, and challenges.

Divorce:

Divorce, even in the best of circumstances, is a painful process. It represents an ending to what has become familiar and normal. I know the sting of divorce. I have seen its ugly head rear up in my mind and in my heart without remorse or concern for my emotional well being or happiness. I know the pain of loss and the resulting low self-esteem at being left behind. It is not a happy time in anyone's life. I would wish that you would never have to experience this in your life, but if you have, I can empathize with your grief and pain.

Divorce can bring out the worst in people: the greed, the envy, the desire to inflict suffering, and often even the joy of hurting someone they once loved. Why is this?

Divorce is about the loss of trust, respect, and love (and even friendship) of your partner. It is often a forgone conclusion, when people are sharing their wedding vows, thinking, "This is wrong, I am making a mistake." But they push on in spite of their inner urgings.

It is important to understand that a successful marriage is not the result of falling in love. It is the result of (there are lots of characteristics, but here are a few of the most important ones):

* commitment
* acceptance
* willingness to change and to grow
* ability to handle differences

Relationships don't fail, people fail in them. A marriage is an entity without feelings, agendas, expectations and problems. These issues are in the people in the relationship. Passion doesn't leave a marriage; it leaves the people in it. So, what can you do? Spend time in honest, non-blaming self-appraisal. Learn about yourself from it.

"We meet ourselves time and time again in a thousand disguises on the path of life."

C. Jung

Summary:

As we move through life, each of us is faced with a variety of situations, circumstances, challenges and relationships that test our patience, resolve, commitment and acceptance. In each of these situations, we always have three options, choices or actions we can take. We can attempt to change the person or circumstance, we can accept it, or we can leave it and move on.

You can attempt to change it. Life is filled with people, events and situations that require us to modify our values and challenge our philosophies—whether it is in our career or personal relationships. During these times when we have difficulty with a corporate policy, a spouse's behavior or a customer's attitudes, we can try to influence them/her/him to change.

It is difficult for many people to accept the reality that people do not change because we want them to or believe they need to, but when and if they choose to. So, if you can't change another person or circumstance, you are left with your next option. You can learn to accept it, or him or her.

Accepting what you dislike, disagree with or oppose is difficult if you are not open and receptive to the following ideas. 1) People change. 2) You are responsible *to* people, not *for* them.

Accepting what you dislike, disagree with or oppose is also difficult if you have any of the following traits. 1) You are living in the past or the future. 2) You have a closed mind. 3) You are stuck in your perceptions, opinions and beliefs. 4) You believe your "way" is the best or only way. 5) Your ego is so in control of your life that, even though you know you are not right, you can't, or refuse to accept what you can't, change. That leaves you with your third and final option—you can leave.

Many people move too quickly to this option when faced with a difficult person or situation. Their patience or acceptance quotient is too low for a peaceful or harmonious coexistence with life. They leave marriages too soon, jobs too quickly and careers or businesses when things begin to get a little difficult or out of hand.

I am not suggesting that people remain in destructive relationships forever, working for Genghis Khan-like supervisors indefinitely, or staying in climates they dislike in order to be a martyr. I am suggesting, however, that many people rush through the first two options too quickly and find that they have left themselves painted into a corner with only one face-saving choice—bailing out.

There are times when leaving is your best choice, given your current set of circumstances and their destructive influence on your self-image, attitudes or life destiny. Only you can decide if you have given yourself and the situation or person adequate time for change, or if you have sincerely tried to put your expectations and prejudices aside and truly accept the person or circumstance. There you have it—change it, accept it or leave it.

Don't sweat the little stuff. What is little stuff? What is big stuff? You are born, big stuff. You die, big stuff. Everything in between is little stuff!

Well, it's back to what *is* little stuff. Little stuff is: (some of you might take issue with my list, but it is my list, so don't get yourself into a twit over it!)

- Getting fired.
- Getting promoted.
- Going broke.
- Winning the lottery.
- Falling in love.
- Falling out of love.
- Graduating from college.
- Retiring.
- Your computer crashing (even if you haven't done a backup in 6 months).
- Losing your hair.
- Losing your mind.
- Taking everything as if it were life or death.
- Losing the biggest sale of your life.
- Losing your business.
- Losing your keys.
- Someone close forgetting your birthday (or any special holiday).
- Getting wrinkles.
- Turning gray.
- Ending a relationship.
- Starting a relationship.

Before this day ends, I guarantee life will give you the opportunity to learn something about yourself.

A comment I often hear from a wide variety of people is, "If I learn just one thing from this person, seminar or life experience, it will be worthwhile."

Life is an interesting and fascinating series of events, processes and growth opportunities. It is what happens to us as we plan the outcomes of our life existence. Life is truly a classroom. In a sense, class begins the day we are born and ends the day we pass from this world to the next. There are no vacations or recesses, and you never graduate.

There is no final exam and there is no pass or fail. You can, however, repeat a grade again and again until you learn the necessary skills or attitudes that the teachers in this class are trying to help you learn.

Each of us is traveling through our very unique life toward a variety of circumstances, events, people, and outcomes. We are bringing these outcomes and people into our lives both unconsciously and consciously.

Some people are good students and learn the necessary lessons the first time they appear, while others are stuck in the same old patterns, life dramas and situations because they fail to bring the learning back to themselves.

You can't quit school, and you must complete each assignment before you get to move on to the next one. There are, however, a number of pop quizzes. Some people refuse to see the learning as theirs. They continuously point their fingers outward toward the other person or event and blame, resent or feel a number of negative emotions such as guilt, jealousy or anger.

Life is a neutral experience. It doesn't care whether you are poor or wealthy, happy or unhappy, educated or ignorant, good looking or ugly, afraid or courageous, from Boston or Atlanta, Catholic or Jewish, single or married, working or retired. It doesn't have opinions. It doesn't judge. It just is.

Class is not about what comes into your life, but about

how you handle it. Success comes to many people. Some handle it well while others do not. Adversity comes to all of us sooner or later. Some people give up, while others use the struggle to get better, wiser or stronger. Everyone has problems—whether in a career, relationships, businesses, with children, customers or spouses.

The opportunity for personal growth or learning can be found in each of life's experiences or teachers. The key to success is to learn to bring all of the learning back to yourself and not to point your finger and blame. You and I don't get to choose the curriculum in our lives or the lives of others, and we certainly don't get to choose how other people should learn their lessons.

Everyone is on a unique path through life into the future. One way to know if you have not yet learned one of life's particular lessons is to observe that which is still in your life. For example, if you are having a relationship problem, there is most likely a relationship lesson that you have not yet learned. If you struggle with a financial lesson, then you have not yet learned a lesson in connection with this issue. The opening line in the all-time bestselling book by M. Scott Peck, *The Road Less Traveled*, states, "Life is difficult." Scott goes on to explain that life is only difficult for people who expect life to be easy!

That's all there is folks... Have a joyful life.

Tim